Published in 2024 by Sunflower Publishing

A CIP catalogue copy of this book can be found in the British Library.

Printed and bound in Scotland by
jamie@weareproductive.co.uk

Sunflower Publishing

CONTROLLING THE FIZZ

CLAIRE STOTT

My name is Jess.

When I first started school
I found it difficult to make friends.

The **busy bustle** of the playground,
the CHITTER-CHATTER from the children,
filled my head with flighty, flying feelings.

At line-up time I found it hard not to reach out to touch Lori's blue fluffy school bag or feel the electric green and red ribbons that held Poppy's pigtails so neatly together.

A loud voice would say

"CAN EVERYONE PLEASE KEEP THEIR HANDS TO THEMSELVES!"

In the classroom, the **BOOMING** DAZZLE from the bright white lights…

…and the swarm of strong smells that brushed my nostrils

made my brain *twirl* and *swirl*.

I didn't like having to sit too long in one place.
It made me feel **ANXIOUS**
I couldn't concentrate or think properly.

My whole body would get hot.

My brain would become mixed up.

It was a bit like when you shake a bottle of fizzy juice and open it.
The bubbles just spill and jump out EVERYWHERE!

THE FIZZ WAS INSIDE OF ME!
When this happened, other children
and the teacher would look sad.
Sometimes they even looked angry at me.

One day my teacher had to take all the other children out of the class to get them away from me.

I always wanted to go home.

My teacher, Mrs Bonnie, was very kind, but because there were so many other children in the class, she found it difficult to help me all the time.

One day a very nice lady called Miss Willow came to work with me. She wasn't a teacher, but she helped the teacher and the other children in the class too.

MISS WILLOW WAS ALWAYS VERY KIND TO ME.

Together we set up a special timetable with pictures on it just for me.

I loved this! It meant that I now knew what was going to happen throughout the day at school.

When each task was done, I could remove it from my timetable.

in between
some TASKS
I HAD
movement
BREAKS

I loved them! We would do lots of
STRETCHING
exercises, and lots of jumping
UP AND DOWN
Sometimes she would roll me over a BIG giant soft ball. I loved this! It really stretched my body out.
Miss Willow was funny too! Sometimes she would say,
"QUICK JESS,
LET'S TRY TO PUSH THIS WALL DOWN!"
We would both push as hard as we could, but it never worked!
We would practise taking deep breaths
in
and
out

Once a week Miss Willow and I would talk
about our feelings and emotions.
At first I hated this, I didn't speak much.

Miss Willow would tell me about her feelings and emotions.
She would tell me about the things that made her happy,
sad, angry, even jealous or scared.

She would show me different pictures of little cartoon bears. They all had different expressions.

One bear looked happy, another bear looked

SHY and **NERVOUS**

There was one bear who looked like some fizz was going to burst out of him!

I liked the bear cards because it meant I could point to a bear that looked like how I was feeling.

Miss Willow and I soon began to imagine situations and stories that might have made the bears make their expressions.

Other days, we would challenge each other to make things with Lego.
Sometimes we would just read or draw.
Before long, I was talking more to Miss Willow about my feelings. I felt safe, because she seemed to understand me, and she always listened.
Together we would make plans to control the **FIZZ** spilling out of my body.
THIS IS TOO HARD
breathe in
breathe out
I CAN DO THIS

I liked this because I didn't like

LOTS of words

when I was getting instructions, it sometimes made the fizz start.

When it was listening time, I would sometimes sit beside Miss Willow. She would press down on my shoulders or my head with her hands. This helped me focus and listen better.
Other times I just fiddled with my fidget toy.
Mrs Bonnie and Miss Willow knew me so well, sometimes they knew when the fizz was going to happen before I did.
They would say...

"JESS time for a break."

My breaks were sometimes in the class. I had my own special corner with a table and chair.

I had a little basket with my book, fidget toy and one other activity that I could do during breaks.

Miss Willow and Mrs Bonnie always spoke with **KIND**, *calm* voices, even when I wasn't speaking kindly to them.

Miss Willow helped me make friends and play with other children in the playground. I still find it hard to share or lose at games. Miss Willow said that was okay as long as I kept trying.

I should always come to her or another adult if I don't feel **safe.**

They will help me explain my

FEELINGS

and give me suggestions how I can feel better.

SOME DAYS I PREFER TO PLAY ON MY OWN AND THAT'S ALSO FINE.

Things also got better at home too. Mum and Dad stopped looking

SAD and **ANGRY**

with me.

Mum and I would do a little timetable in the mornings when we were having breakfast.

I made pictures myself. This was fun! It also made me feel **safe** because I knew what my day was going to look like.

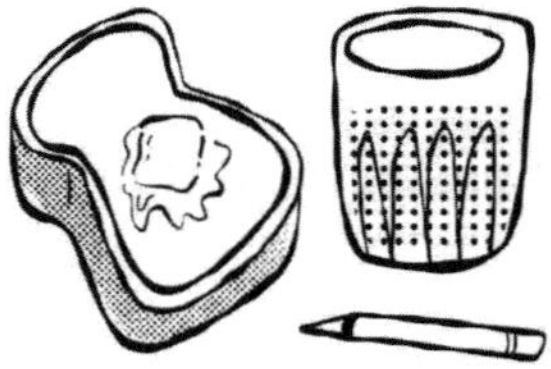

I didn't get sent to my room as much.

When the **FIZZ** happened, Mum and Dad would stay calm and help me.

We would talk to each other about our feelings and emotions.

WE DID A LOT OF
REALLY COOL STUFF
TOGETHER
We still do.

When I was in Primary 3, I even started some after school clubs. Art, and Drama, but my **favourite** club was **BASKETBALL!**

He told me it was okay if I just wanted to sit and watch the children play, but I could join in any time if I felt like it.
By the second week I started to join in. By the third week I didn't even want or need Mum to stay.
Sam is a really cool coach, some days I just want to sit in a corner and play with my fidget toy.
Sam is always okay with that. He always gives me a high-five!

I'M NOW IN PRIMARY 7!

I'm almost as tall as coach Sam.

When **summer** term begins, Miss Willow and I are going to visit the High School one afternoon, once a week.

We will meet some adults that do the same job as Miss Willow They will help me settle into High School life. I'll get to look around some of the classrooms and take some photos to show Mum and Dad.

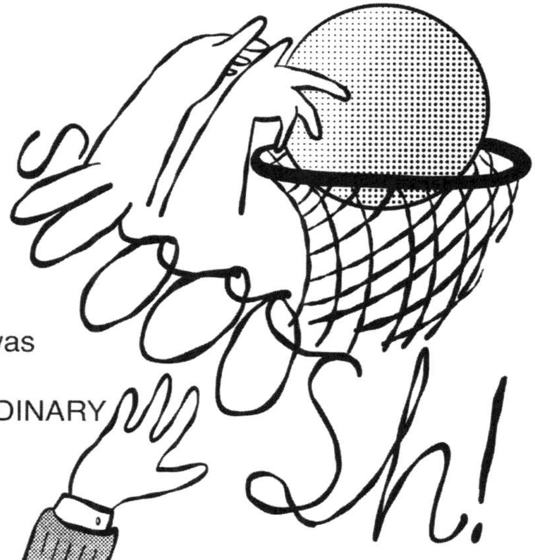

Miss Willow once told me that it was good to have some ***FIZZ*** as it can make me do EXTRAORDINARY things with my life,

but it was important to know the things that I can do to stop the ***FIZZ*** bursting out.

I FEEL HAPPY MOST OF THE TIME.

I have many kind friends.
My special friend is Lori.

I still have the blue fluffy school bag that she bought for my birthday when we were in Primary 2.

The **FIZZ** is still there, but I'm not as scared of it.

I have learned to be the boss of it.

I LIKE BEING ME!
I THINK IT'S COOL THAT WE'RE ALL DIFFERENT.
I try to find my own happiness.
I don't worry if it's not the same as someone else's happiness.
THE WORLD WOULD BE SO BORING IF WE WERE ALL THE SAME.

If Jess was in your class, what could you do to show your friendship?

Can you remember a time when you felt anxious or overwhelmed?

If so, what things did you do to help yourself?

Do you have a trusted adult in your life that you can talk to about your thoughts and feelings?
1.
2.
3.
Why is it important to respect each other's differences?

MY DOODLE PAGE

*You can colour in all the pages!

About Us

Writer

Claire has worked for over ten years as a Pupil Support Assistant in an Edinburgh Primary School.

She has 2 children, Sam and Lori. She lives in the Blackford Area of the city with her husband Grant and their Chihuahua “Willow.”

They enjoy walks around her favourite places, Bruntsfield Links and Meadows.

Illustrator

Cassandra is a British American artist living in Scotland with her daughter Lottie and their energetic dog, Astro.

Cassandra creates illustrations for books, socks, chocolate wrappers, universities, shop fronts, Timberland boots and private commissions. When she was 8 years old she knew she wanted to be An Artist.

www.cassandraharrison.co.uk

Printed in Great Britain
by Amazon

61697047R00020